DAVID WILLIAMSON is Australia's best-known and most widely performed playwright. His first full-length play, *The Coming of Stork*, was presented at La Mama Theatre in 1970 and was followed by *The Removalists, Don's Party, The Department, The Club, Travelling North, The Perfectionist, Sons of Cain, Emerald City, Top Silk, Money and Friends, Brilliant Lies, Sanctuary, Dead White Males, After the Ball, Corporate Vibes, Face to Face, Rupert, Nearer the Gods, Odd Man Out, Sorting out Rachel, The Big Time*, and *Family Values*. He has had over fifty plays produced. His plays have been translated into many languages and performed internationally, including major productions in London, Los Angeles, New York and Washington. As a screenwriter, Williamson has brought his own plays to the screen, including *The Removalists, Don's Party, The Club, Travelling North* and *Emerald City*, along with his original screenplays for feature films, including *Libido, Petersen, Gallipoli, Phar Lap, The Year of Living Dangerously* and *Balibo*. The adaptation of his play *Face to Face*, directed by Michael Rymer, won the Panavision Spirit Award for Independent Film at the Santa Barbara International Film Festival. Williamson was the first person outside Britain to receive the George Devine Award (for *The Removalists*). His many awards include twelve Australian Writers' Guild AWGIE Awards, five Australian Film Institute Awards for Best Screenplay, and in 1996 the United Nations Association of Australia Media Peace Award. In 2005 he was awarded the Richard Lane Award for services to the Australian Writers' Guild. In 2011 he was given the lifetime achievement award by the Sydney Critics Circle. In 2015 he was awarded the NSW Premier's Literary Awards special achievement award. In 2021 his memoir, *Home Truths*, was published by Harper Collins. David has received four honorary doctorates, been made an Officer of the Order of Australia and named one of Australia's Living National Treasures. He lives on Queensland's Sunshine Coast with his writer wife, Kristin Williamson.

Guy Edmonds (left) and Matt Minto in Crunch Time *at The Ensemble Theatre. (Photo: Prudence Upton)*

CRUNCH TIME

DAVID WILLIAMSON

CURRENCY PRESS
The performing arts publisher

CURRENCY PLAYS

First published in 2022
by Currency Press Pty Ltd,
PO Box 2287, Strawberry Hills, NSW, 2012, Australia
enquiries@currency.com.au
www.currency.com.au

Typeset by Brighton Gray for Currency Press.
Cover image shows Guy Edmonds and John Wood.
Cover photo by Prudence Upton. Cover design by Lisa White.

A catalogue record for this book is available from the National Library of Australia

Contents

Currency Press acknowledges the Traditional Owners of the Country on which we live and work. We pay our respects to all Aboriginal and Torres Strait Islander Elders, past and present.

Matt Minto (left), Di Craig and John Wood in CRUNCH TIME *at The Ensemble Theatre. (Photo: Prudence Upton)*

Introduction

David Williamson is Australia's most popular and prolific playwright. Over the past 50 years he has written roughly a play a year, as well as half as many screenplays. His work has enriched the coffers of all our state theatre companies as well as others such as Nimrod and Sydney's Ensemble Theatre, where the annual Williamson remains the hot ticket of the subscription season.

His plays have been presented in London and the US, and a number of them, including *The Removalists, Don's Party, The Club, Travelling North* and *Emerald City* have been made into successful films.

Few playwrights have ever enjoyed such a long love affair with a theatre-going public. Fashions quickly change and audiences crave novelty. Incoming artistic directors are keen to set their stamp on the repertoire and woo their subscribers with shows that reflect the latest trends. Room has to be made each season for new writers (who are happy to elbow older ones out of the way) with a heavy emphasis now on ethnic diversity and gender parity ... A lot has changed in the theatre since David Williamson landed on the boards of La Mama in the 1960s.

And yet he has endured. What is the secret of his enduring success? I well remember 'the shock of the new' when I read *The Removalists* back in 1971. Here was a fresh, raw and gutsy play that caught the tang of the Australian vernacular with an authenticity we hadn't heard since Ray Lawler's *Summer of the Seventeenth Doll*. Audiences hooted with surprise and delight at the unapologetic crudeness and violence of it; this was theatre with the gloves off, and a very different experience to the decorous doses of culture being doled out by the Melbourne Theatre Company or Sydney's Old Tote.

It was significant that Williamson's early plays premiered in rough makeshift spaces such as Melbourne's La Mama and Sydney's Nimrod and Jane Street. Only once their popularity and box office success was established did Williamson's plays make their way to the state-subsidised main stages.

Williamson homed in on aspects of 'the ugly Australian' that polite society preferred to ignore. The police force had never been presented in such an unglamorous light as in *The Removalists*. Here was Sergeant Simonds, the archetypal lazy, corrupt and inefficient copper beating up young Kenny, the tradie who won't stand for being pushed around by authority.

Don's Party gave us images of Australian males at play in all their drunken sexist splendour, accompanied by a sardonic commentary from the sidelines by the women in their lives. I was reminded of a lunch I was invited to in suburban Melbourne in the early '70s.

The men were all beefy, hairy, intellectual and arty lefties who were served a rather splendid lunch by their female partners. Lunch done, the host announced 'Okay, men, let's be off to the footy. The girls can stay behind and do the washing up.'

The bullish, sexist patriarchal figure we first meet in Sergeant Simonds recurs in various guises, sometimes as a figure of fun. He reaches his apogee in Jock, the devious domineering bullshit artist in *The Club*. He may have his counterparts in American and English drama, but you won't find any as funny as Jock. It is immensely satisfying to watch the old fraud setting himself up for an almighty tumble. The same figure will appear in a more moderate version in later Williamson plays, notably Frank in *Travelling North*, and we can find a flicker of him in Steve in *Crunch Time*.

We can see that Steve has been neither the ideal husband nor the ideal father. He belongs to that generation of self-made men for whom work was almost all-consuming. Wife and family fitted in around it. With his focus on sporting prowess and relative disdain for intellectual and artistic pursuits, he is shaping up as the familiar ocker figure. He is salvaged somewhat by his devotion to Helen, and through her and her rendition of a piece of Bach, he has a dim vision of something better. There is a measure of sensitivity in Steve after all, and we are prompted to view him as a product of the society that made him this way—a society that endorses a toxic masculinity and philistinism.

It's the kind of society that gags men from expressing tender feelings, in fact derides them for having any. Baffled by not having the language to communicate with his son Luke, Steve has opted for silent withdrawal. And so the curse is passed on to Luke who is ill-equipped to express or value himself.

Steve is the last in that line of domineering patriarchs who intrigue Williamson and provide him fertile ground for satire. Rupert Murdoch cops a healthy serve in the play named after him and I'd like to have seen what David might have done with the Packer dynasty had Tommy Murphy not pipped him at the post with his *Packer and Sons*. Whatever his faults, Steve is given a free kick by contracting cancer, which not only makes him a figure of genuine pathos, but also enforces on him a degree of self-reflection he might otherwise never have undertaken. The big showdown between Steve and Luke (scene 23) is, I think, one of the finest David has written and is a beautifully sustained and organic catharsis.

Alongside his forensic examination of the Australian male psyche, David has remained fiercely contemporary. Whereas other Australian playwrights have allowed themselves to dip into this country's rich history and foreign landscapes as well, David's plays are all set pretty well now, mainly in Sydney and Melbourne, frequently exploiting the uneasy nexus between the two.

The only exception is the play before this one, *Nearer the Gods*, dealing with Sir Isaac Newton and Halley's Comet—a remarkable departure from his familiar turf.

Just as earlier audiences rejoiced at Williamson's deconstruction of an alpha-male society, later audiences have been delighted by his commentaries on middle-class suburbia, its aspirations and hypocrisies, its obsession with money and real estate.

Familiarity and a sense of ownership are a very large part of Williamson's appeal. Entertaining and rewarding as it may be to watch and listen to a play by Alan Ayckbourn, Tom Stoppard or Edward Albee, there is an extra level of engagement with characters we know as well as we know the people next door. We feel these plays are for us and about us.

David's location of his plays in our immediate neighbourhood is compounded by his commitment as a social commentator, seeking out issues that pertain to here and now, whether it be politics, family issues of loyalty and betrayal or more focussed debate such as his critique of post-modernism in *Dead White Males*.

In *Crunch Time* the pressing issue is the debate around assisted dying. But this is no dry piece of polemic. It is played out in very human terms by people, like many in the audience, who have qualms, fears and reservations. The resolution in this play is a moving and generous one. We have witnessed acts of brutality, pain and reconciliation. But we are not sent home with a comfortable assurance that all has been resolved. People have just done the best they can under the circumstances, as we all must, leading Helen to conclude, 'All is more or less well with the world.'

John Bell
September 2021

Crunch Time was first produced at the Ensemble Theatre, Sydney, on 16 February 2020, with the following cast:

LUKE	Guy Edmonds
JIMMY	Matt Minto
STEVE	John Wood
HELEN	Diane Craig
LAUREN	Emma Palmer
SUSY	Megan Drury

Director, Mark Kilmurry
Assistant Director, Janine Watson
Set and Costume Designer, Lauren Peters
Lighting Designer, Nicholas Higgins
Sound Realiser, Anthony Lorenz
Stage Managers, Brooke Kiss and Stephanie Lindwall
Costume Supervisor, Renata Beslik

CHARACTERS

LUKE CAMPBELL, 40

JIMMY CAMPBELL, 38

STEVE CAMPBELL, 66

HELEN CAMPBELL, early 60s

LAUREN CAMPBELL, Luke's wife

SUSY CAMPBELL, Jimmy's wife

SETTING

Various locations around Sydney.

Matt Minto and Megan Drury in Crunch Time *at The Ensemble Theatre. (Photo: Prudence Upton)*

ACT ONE

LUKE CAMPBELL, *40, is in his office dressed in a shabby ill-fitting suit and heavy glasses, looking every bit the computer nerd. He sits at his desk staring at his computer as he shifts from bar charts to pie charts to tables of figures. His office door is flung open. His brother* JIMMY, *38, by contrast impeccably dressed and charismatic, flings open the door, and storms angrily in waving a folder.*

JIMMY: What the fuck Luke!

> LUKE *looks up and considers his brother calmly.*

LUKE: I don't think it's a wise move.

JIMMY: This has been researched and costed to within an inch of its life—it's the best opportunity we've had in years.

LUKE: Too risky.

JIMMY: Have you bothered to read this?!

> *He waves the folder.*

LUKE: Many times.

JIMMY: [*furious*] Then read it again! The risk factors are all there and our research shows they're not significant! Not significant!

LUKE: That's what you said about China.

JIMMY: Oh Jesus! Not China again. Not fucking China again! We can't work this way Luke! If we want the firm to grow, risk is part of the equation, and when the risk is small and the upside huge like this is—

> *He waves the folder angrily again.*

Anyone. ANYONE! But a BOWL OF FUCKING JELLY would shout hallelujah and jump at the chance.

LUKE: [*calmly stubborn*] It's too risky.

> LUKE *looks as if he's about to physically assault his brother, but then turns on his heel and storms out.*

SCENE TWO

STEVE CAMPBELL, *66, an impressive looking and assertive man, is standing by the window of his home in Potts Point looking out over the harbour. There's a knock at the door and* JIMMY, *his son, in his late 30s, handsome and charismatic, enters. He's on edge, which is unusual as normally he's cool and unruffled.*

STEVE: You said there's a problem?

JIMMY: Dad, it was a nice thought that Luke and I could run your firm together, but—

STEVE: Disagreements can be healthy. Clear the air. Lead to new decisions.

JIMMY: Dad, do you want your firm to survive and grow?

STEVE: Jimmy, he knows the nuts and bolts of the business far better than you do—

JIMMY: Sure, but what's the use of making world class precision instruments if he sends buyers into deep REM sleep when he starts talking about them!

STEVE: That consultant I brought in to sharpen his presentation? Charlie said it had improved him.

JIMMY: It has. It takes less time for our clients to realise he's still alive.

STEVE: I'll get the guy in again.

JIMMY: It's past that Dad. We're shouting at each other every second day.

STEVE: Yeah, Charlie told me.

JIMMY: Dad, Luke is a gifted engineer, but I just can't work with him.

> STEVE *looks at his son and nods.*

SCENE THREE

Later in his living room, STEVE *is back staring out the window as his wife* HELEN *talks to him. She is in her early 60s, elegant and still beautiful.*

STEVE: It was always my dream. Something I'd created against all odds, being taken into the future by my two hugely talented sons.

HELEN: A lovely dream. But it was never going to work.

STEVE: I'm going to have to let one of them go.

HELEN: Which one?

STEVE: I don't know.

HELEN: Make sure you handle it well.

STEVE: Whichever way it goes I want to make sure emotions don't enter into it.

HELEN: My dear, emotions can't help but enter into it.

SCENE FOUR

LAUREN, *the slim, attractive but rather febrile wife of* LUKE, *Steve's other son, stares at* LUKE. LUKE, *in his late 30s, is certainly not as charismatic as his younger brother Jimmy. And unlike Jimmy, who has great fashion sense,* LUKE *looks as if he collected his wardrobe from a charity shop.*

LAUREN: A letter? He fired you in a letter?

> LUKE, *quietly furious, nods.*

No warning of any kind?

> LUKE *shakes his head and hands her the letter. She reads the letter.*

Well at least he's made it clear your share of his inheritance isn't at risk.

LUKE: [*staring at her*] You think that makes it all fine?

LAUREN: There's a hell of a lot of money involved.

> LUKE *stares at her.*

LUKE: And that makes it fine by you?

LAUREN: There's a hell of a lot of money involved.

> LUKE *gives her a withering stare and looks away.*

SCENE FIVE

HELEN *stares at* STEVE.

HELEN: You didn't talk to him first?

STEVE: I didn't want emotions to enter into it.

HELEN: [*with sarcasm*] That's been spectacularly successful then hasn't it?

> *She holds up a letter.*

He sends us a letter that he wants no further communication with either of us. Either of us. Ever.

STEVE: Call him. Say it was nothing to do with you.

HELEN: I tried. He hung up. And they've got our grandchild on the way!

STEVE: He'll change his mind.

HELEN: Luke? Once Luke's made up his mind, no force on earth can change it.

SCENE SIX

LAUREN *looks at* LUKE *furious. She has a copy of the letter he sent his father in her hand.*

LAUREN: Your mother called.

LUKE: Yeah.

LAUREN: Did you tell her you want nothing to do with your father or her.

LUKE: Yes.

LAUREN: Ever?

LUKE: Yes.

LAUREN: Luke that's crazy!

LUKE: He fired me by letter?

LAUREN: I'm four bloody months pregnant and you've just ensured you get cut out of his will.

LUKE: Couldn't care less.

LAUREN: Couldn't care less?

LUKE: I'm a good engineer. I'll do fine.

LAUREN: Whatever you earn it'll be peanuts compared with half of your father's estate. Make it up with your father!

LUKE: No way!

> *She shakes her head and storms off.*

SCENE SEVEN

STEVE *is in his living room again with* HELEN. *It is six years later. She shows him a photo on his iPhone.*

HELEN: Aren't they sweet?

> STEVE *glances angrily at the image.*

STEVE: That's good enough for you?

HELEN: It's better than nothing.

STEVE: They're my grandkids. And we've both only ever seen them on your bloody iPhone. And only then because Lauren sends them to you behind Luke's back.

HELEN: I miss them desperately too.

STEVE: It's nearly six years now and he still won't even talk to you!

HELEN: I must admit I didn't think he was going to hold out that long.

STEVE: The decision I made turns out to be the right one. Under Jimmy, the firm's going ahead in leaps and bounds.

HELEN: You think that makes Luke feel any better?

STEVE: I've written three long and heartfelt letters of apology and nothing back! Nothing.

HELEN: It's harsh. I have to admit.

STEVE: If grudge holding were an Olympic sport he'd have a bloody gold medal.

> STEVE *winces with pain.* HELEN *notices, concerned.*

HELEN: Have you been to the doctor about that pain?

STEVE: It's nothing.

HELEN: Go.

STEVE: Alright!

HELEN: Go! Tomorrow.

STEVE: Okay, okay!

SCENE EIGHT

LAUREN *is confronting* LUKE.

LUKE: I don't want to see her.

LAUREN: That's stupid Luke. She didn't approve of what your father did.

LUKE: She didn't stop him doing it, did she?

LAUREN: She says it's important.

LUKE: I don't want to see anyone from that family.

LAUREN: That family. It's your family. Your mother is coming here and you're going to be polite to her! Right?

SCENE NINE

HELEN *confronts her son and daughter-in-law.*

HELEN: You father's got pancreatic cancer. If he's lucky he's got six months to live.

There's a silence.

Six months at the most.

There's a silence.

LAUREN: That's terrible Helen. I'm so sorry.

LUKE: I'm sorry.

Beat.

For you.

HELEN *stares at him.*

HELEN: He's going to die an excruciating death. And you don't give a damn?

LUKE: I'm sorry for what you're going to go through.

LAUREN: Luke? Your father's dying.

LUKE: And I'm sorry. For Mum.

HELEN: I couldn't have believed that any son of mine could be so callous.

She goes to walk out.

LUKE: [*anguished*] Mum, it's not just what happened seven years ago. I've been number two son with Dad all my life. He never cared about me! Why should I suddenly care about him now!

HELEN: Luke you're being ridiculous. Your father loved both of you.

LUKE: [*bursting out*] Bullshit! Everything Jimmy did was gold, I was just the klutz who embarrassed him.

HELEN: That's utter nonsense.

LUKE: You just didn't want to see it so you didn't.

LAUREN: Luke, whatever. Your father's dying. Move on.

LUKE: It's not that easy!

HELEN: [*to* LUKE] Your father was always hugely proud of your achievements. At school, at university.

LUKE: What really rated with Dad were Jimmy's cricket centuries and swimming records.

HELEN: He was proud of you both. He really was.

LUKE: Yeah, in a pat on the head sort of way. He had no idea of what I was going through in my school years and he didn't care.

LAUREN: Luke, your father is dying.

LUKE: He never gave a shit about me!

HELEN: Your father was never the most sensitive man in the world, but I can't believe you didn't know he loved you and was proud of you.

LUKE: I tried to tell him I was going through hell at that bloody macho rugger bugger school he made me go to and his response? 'Tough it out and stop acting like a wimp.'

HELEN: I tried to get you out of there.

LUKE: But he wouldn't budge. I was near suicidal

HELEN: Luke, you've got grievances. And a lot of them are justified. Talk to your father about them before it's too late.

LUKE: All he was interested in was his bloody business. Did he even love you?

HELEN: Yes, always.

LUKE: How would you know? He was never there.

HELEN: When he said he was going to make better and more innovative precision instruments than the Germans he was laughed at. To prove them wrong he hardly slept for ten years.

LUKE: And you had to sacrifice your career in the process.

HELEN: I wasn't ever going to do better than second cello in one of our minor orchestras.

LUKE: You've had your own string quartet for years and years. You still get work.

HELEN: Mainly at weddings for next to nothing. Luke, most of us have to face some very bleak moments of truth in their life. I finally had to face mine. I'd spent twenty thousand hours of my life slavishly devoted to meticulous practice and discovered that I was good, but not quite good enough.

Beat.

You're carrying this war with your father too far. If you let him die without even saying goodbye it would just be unspeakably cruel. And frankly I'd never forgive you.

HELEN *looks at her son. Emotional. She turns and leaves.* LAUREN *waits until she's out of earshot and turns on* LUKE *angrily.*

LAUREN: How do you think he's going to react to this? You cut him out, he's going to do the same to you.

LUKE: That's all that matters to you, isn't it? His bloody money!

SCENE TEN

STEVE *is furious as he talks to* HELEN, JIMMY *and Jimmy's wife* SUSY.

STEVE: [*to* HELEN] He's not getting a bloody cent!

HELEN: He's going to take it as another huge sign of rejection.

STEVE: He couldn't hate me any more than he does.

SUSY: He doesn't hate you.

STEVE *looks at her.*

He's hurt, he's angry, but at another level—

STEVE: What?

SUSY: I think he's still craving for the approval and love he thinks you never gave him.

JIMMY: Susy, save your psychologizing for your clients.

STEVE: [*to* SUSY] I never stopped giving him approval.

HELEN: For his exam results. Nothing else.

STEVE: Apart from his exam results, it wasn't easy to find things to praise him about. He was hopeless socially.

HELEN: And you never stopped criticising him for it.

STEVE: It's not as if I didn't care. My heart used to bleed for him when he was a little tacker watching him trying to make friends and being so hopeless at it. I just didn't know what to do.

HELEN: You could've put your arm around his shoulders. Told him it was okay.

STEVE: Okay, I was never good at the huggy stuff.

JIMMY: Mum, he was a pain in the butt. Too bloody sensitive about everything. And he's behaving like an absolute bastard right now.

SUSY: [*to* STEVE] He desperately needed to feel you loved him.

STEVE: I did. If he couldn't see that it's his bloody fault.

HELEN *sighs.*

HELEN: Understanding other people was never one of your strong points.

STEVE: I understand people just as well as anyone else.

HELEN: My love, I've spent half my life phoning people to apologize after you insulted them at their dinner parties.

STEVE: That's rubbish!

HELEN: You're a brilliant innovative engineer, but your people skills are somewhere between Peter Dutton and The Grinch who stole Christmas.

STEVE: Who have I ever insulted?

HELEN: When you found out my friend Naomi was a lesbian, you asked whether she had a bad relationship with her father.

STEVE: She probably did.

HELEN: And you asked Glenda who was having chemotherapy if super short hair was a new fashion. And just yesterday you complimented that woman with anorexia on how thin she was.

STEVE: Everyone puts their foot in it sometimes.

HELEN: Not quite as often as you. How would you suggest we handle it Susy?

JIMMY: Mum, don't bloody well encourage her. I forget to put out the rubbish and I'm staging a passive aggressive rebellion against sharing the housework.

SUSY: I'd suggest Steve writes him a letter—

STEVE: I've written him three already. He doesn't reply.

SUSY: Tell him the truth. You're deeply hurt by his reaction. Then say that despite this, he's your son, that you love him, and that you're not going to be vindictive and he's still getting his full inheritance.

STEVE: No way! I'm changing my will and that's it.

SUSY: If you send the letter and he still doesn't respond, then I'd agree. Cut him out entirely. But give him that one last chance.

HELEN: Do it Steve. If you care for me at all, do it.

There's a silence. He looks around at them.

SCENE ELEVEN

SUSY *is holding an iPhone in one hand and staring at* JIMMY.

SUSY: You said she didn't go to Kuala Lumpur with you.

JIMMY: Where did you get that?

SUSY: Unless you're totally stupid you must have realized that given that nothing escapes anybody's notice in the days of Facebook and

Instagram there was a chance, and a pretty good chance, that this would find its way to me.

JIMMY: Susy—

SUSY: What exactly is it I'm lacking Jimmy?

JIMMY: Nothing.

SUSY: You were enough for me. So much so that I would never have dreamed of jeopardizing what we had for an occasional wild fuck.

JIMMY: It was a bit of unfinished business.

SUSY: Unfinished business?

JIMMY: It's over. Totally over. And this is the last time. It'll never happen again. Truly.

SUSY: I used to congratulate myself that we weren't like the other marriages we saw. Clashing temperaments, bitter arguments, friends falling out of love with each other. We weren't like that. Never. And then. Vanessa. Vanessa?

JIMMY: Susy, don't do this.

SUSY: My husband and my best friend. Everything I believed was real was suddenly a pathetic and naive illusion.

JIMMY: Susy, stop it.

SUSY: But tears, sincere apologies. Begging for forgiveness. And I was so desperate to claim my perfect world back I fell for it—I forgave you.

JIMMY: Susy, please.

SUSY: Then Tracy? The tough little tart you told me you couldn't stand. Gave you all sorts of bother at work. Always on the point of firing her. Sure.

JIMMY: Susy.

SUSY: And why did this happen? She came into your office and broke down in tears and said she'd have to leave because she was crazily in love with you.

JIMMY: Do you think I'm proud of it?

SUSY: That makes it all okay? You're not proud so it's okay?

JIMMY: I'm not! I'm really not!

SUSY: What is it with you Jimmy? Are you such a narcissist that you can't resist offering to light up their grim little lives with your charm and charisma.

JIMMY: Susy, it was just a slip. One last mistake. Its all over.

SUSY: Jimmy, it's one mistake too many. There's a line. You don't really know it's there, but it's there all the time and you don't know quite where it is until that line is crossed. It's over Jimmy. The line's been crossed.

JIMMY: Susy that's crazy.

SUSY: Did you really think that your conquests would be happy to have you in bed with them in some hotel for an hour once a week? You didn't think perhaps they might be wanting the thing I wanted. A man to share a life with? From the minute you unhooked their bra you had just started on a course that was going to lead to anger and despair for two women. You didn't think of that?

JIMMY: I'm sorry.

SUSY: The truth is you probably didn't. You probably thought how generous you were to be bestowing the great gift of you on another grateful woman.

JIMMY: This is the last mistake I am ever going to make. I swear.

SUSY: It crossed the line Jimmy. I didn't know it would until it happened but it crossed the line. Our marriage is over.

JIMMY: That's crazy. I love you.

SUSY: For the first time in your life you're about to feel something you've inflicted on too many others. Get used to it.

    She turns and leaves.

SCENE TWELVE

HELEN *waits for* LUKE *at his workplace. She looks at her watch. Looks around. Sips some coffee.* LUKE *appears. He looks at her warily.*

LUKE: Do you want to come through to the office?

HELEN: Did you get your father's letter?

LUKE: Yes.

HELEN: I hope you appreciate it was a great effort for him.

LUKE: I was surprised. Can we go to the off—

HELEN: You haven't responded.

LUKE: No.

HELEN: Don't you think it's pretty extraordinary that he's still going to give you your full inheritance?

LUKE: I was surprised.

HELEN: But you're going to do nothing?

LUKE: I'm going to write back.

HELEN: Write!

LUKE: I'm going to thank him and tell him that I don't want it.

HELEN: Luke. You're being stubborn to the point of crazy.

LUKE: Mum, believe it or not, I really don't want the money.

HELEN: How does Lauren feel?

LUKE: She wants it. For sure. The only reason she's not divorcing me now is that it makes more sense to wait until I have Dad's money, then divorce me and take half.

HELEN: I don't think she's that calculating.

LUKE: You think it was an accident she became a lot more interested in me when she found out who my father was.

HELEN: I don't think it was like that.

LUKE: No? You remember the first time I brought her to meet the family?

HELEN: She was nervous and got drunk.

LUKE: So it's all fine that I go out the back and see Jimmy and her kissing?

HELEN: She was hugely ashamed and so was Jimmy.

LUKE: She wasn't ashamed. Just embarrassed that she was caught. But that's fine. She was just being logical. If she was going to marry money then why not Jimmy and not the dork.

HELEN: You were never a dork.

LUKE: My father thinks I was.

HELEN: Well I didn't. If I had a favourite back then it was probably you.

> LUKE *stares in surprise.*

LUKE: Why? Because I was more vulnerable?

HELEN: Yes. But right now you're making it hard for anyone to love you.

> *Beat.*

Go and talk to your father.

LUKE: Mum, there's no point. Tell him to give my share to cancer research.

> HELEN *looks at her stubborn son and sighs.*

SCENE THIRTEEN

HELEN, STEVE *and* JIMMY *are together in* STEVE'*s living room.*

STEVE: [*with his hands on his head*] Jimmy. How much grief have you caused in how many lives because you can't keep your dick in your trousers!

    Beat.

You're an idiot son. Susy's a gem.

JIMMY: Can we move on? You said you had something you wanted me to do.

    STEVE *looks at* JIMMY.

STEVE: Yes.

    He looks at him and then at HELEN.

It's a very aggressive cancer. From here on in I'll start to go rapidly downhill. I want it to end before I become … unrecognizable.

JIMMY: Euthanasia?

STEVE: Euthanasia is hopeless. I want voluntary assisted dying. It's legal in Victoria but in this state, where the government is controlled by religious fanatics, I'd need to be in a state where I'm a human skeleton with a face like a skull and no control over my bowel movements before the doctors are allowed to finish me.

JIMMY: It's not going to make us feel any the worse about you.

STEVE: Jimmy, can you get the fact that I can't stand the thought of being remembered like that.

    Beat.

I need Nembutal. But it's hard to get.

JIMMY: It's illegal?

STEVE: In this bloody state, very much so.

HELEN: There's a large fine if you're caught importing it.

STEVE: You'll have to travel. I can't any more.

    JIMMY *frowns.*

HELEN: I offered.

STEVE: If anyone's going to prison it can't be you.

JIMMY: Thanks

STEVE: It's a lot to ask, I know.

JIMMY: Travel? Where to?

STEVE: From my online research, it looks like the most promising place is Peru.

JIMMY: Peru?

STEVE: The drug's still used in the veterinary industry to put down animals.

JIMMY: Do you have any addresses?

STEVE: No. You'll have to do some research. But it is available. In liquid form.

JIMMY: And you'd drink it?

STEVE: I want it injected. It's quicker, more effective. I'll have home pain relief in a month or so according to my doctor, so you just detach the syringe driver and inject straight into the line.

JIMMY: We inject?

STEVE: When I give you the signal.

HELEN: I couldn't.

JIMMY: If we assist a suicide …?

STEVE: You'd be breaking the law and liable to ten years in prison. But you won't be at risk. I'll write a note saying I injected myself.

JIMMY: Wouldn't it be better if you did?

STEVE: Not sure I could handle that final moment of decision myself.

HELEN: I couldn't.

STEVE: We'll talk about this later. First thing is getting the Nembutal.

JIMMY: Getting it through customs. Is it a large fine?

STEVE: Not in the quantities you're bringing in.

JIMMY: But still—

STEVE: Put a false label on it. It's highly unlikely you'll be caught.

There's a silence.

A final act of mercy. Of respect. Of … hopefully … love, by the two people I care most about.

There's another silence.

Please. Don't reduce me to the indignity of a half human.

He looks at them.

Hey. It's not tragic. We all die. Some a lot sooner than I will. I've been blessed with the miracle of existence. One sperm out of millions hit the egg and here I am. Descended in an unbroken line from our ancestral amoeba. The chances of all that happening are trillions of billions to one. I won an incredibly unlikely lottery. Okay I'm going out a little sooner than I'd hoped but I'd much rather have had the life I've had than never existed at all. For a brief moment in time I was here. Hallelujah.

JIMMY: Do you want this to happen Mum?

HELEN: If your father wants it then I want it. I just can't do it. I can't even be there when it happens.

JIMMY: What time frame are we talking about?

STEVE: Not long. A month, two months before it really starts to bite.

> JIMMY *hesitates.*

Jimmy, I haven't asked all that much of you up to now. I need this to happen.

> *There's a silence.*

SCENE FOURTEEN

LUKE *answers the doorbell and* LAUREN *enters looking very chic.*

LUKE: Good conference?

LAUREN: Not sure whether conferences ever achieve anything much.

LUKE: Well this one wouldn't because there was no legal conference in Port Douglas this week. There hasn't been one there all year.

LAUREN: I just needed to get away by myself for a while.

LUKE: By yourself?

> *He takes out his iPhone. He shows her a photo.*

Looks like you had a very chummy meal at Nautilus with Murray Hendon.

LAUREN: He just happened to be there buying a getaway.

LUKE: A getaway? He's got six houses scattered over the globe already hasn't he?

LAUREN: Nothing is happening. You're paranoid. He was there buying a house!

> LUKE *attacks from another direction.*

LUKE: I've decided that my share of Dad's money is going to cancer research.

LAUREN *stares at him.*

LAUREN: Are you totally fucking crazy!

LUKE: I actually feel pretty good about it.

LAUREN: Have you thought what we could do with that sort of money?

LUKE: Like what?

LAUREN: Wouldn't you like to quit what you're doing?

LUKE: I love what I'm doing.

LAUREN: Well I don't. Crafting contracts to make sure the rich get super rich and getting only a dribble of cash for my efforts.

LUKE: Pretty healthy dribble. What does Murray Hendon pay you as a retainer?

LAUREN: For God's sake go and make it up with your dad! If you keep acting like a lunatic, I'm out of here.

LUKE: Out of here?

LAUREN: When was the last time we had good sex?

LUKE: Money would magically restore our libidos?

LAUREN: We'd have time for each other again.

LUKE: Our kids? You'd put them through a breakup?

LAUREN: I don't want to Luke. But I don't want the life we have now either.

LUKE: What is wrong with the life we lead now? We've got six-figure salaries, beautiful house? What kind of amazing life is it you want to lead?

LAUREN: Quit my God-awful job. Buy a beautiful old farmhouse in Tuscany or Umbria or Puglia and paint, and sculpt, and read the books I'm desperate to read but never get time. Drink great wines and eat food at restaurants where the chefs are artists.

LUKE: A life of total self indulgence?

LAUREN: And why the hell not?

LUKE: Because I'd be bored stiff in two weeks.

LAUREN: You've got such narrow fucking horizons!

LUKE: I'm not going to fake feelings I don't have so you can live like a pampered princess.

LAUREN: I've only got my one moment on earth and I don't intend to waste it. Go and make it up with your father or I really am out of here.

SCENE FIFTEEN

We're in JIMMY *'s living room. Spacious, affluent.* JIMMY *sits in a lounge chair, looking at* LUKE *who is sitting opposite him looking agitated. He gets up.*

LUKE: You wanted to talk? Okay, talk.

JIMMY: You're not even going to talk to Dad before he dies.

LUKE: There's no point.

JIMMY: He's your fucking father!

LUKE: We've got nothing to say to each other.

JIMMY: Okay, you don't give a shit about Dad. But how could you do that to Mum?

LUKE: I'm sorry about Mum.

JIMMY: She couldn't have been a better mother to you. And you weren't easy for her mate. Easy for any of us. You were as prickly as hell.

LUKE: Was I expected to be super friendly when I knew you and Dad were always laughing at me behind my back.

JIMMY: Don't be so fucking paranoid!

LUKE: One day my best friends arrived to play Dungeons and Dragons and you said 'here comes the nerd herd'. And Dad laughed his head off.

JIMMY: Mate, face it. You were obsessed. For three years all you could talk about was wood elfs, shadow demons and wardukes.

LUKE: A game of intelligence and imagination. All you and Dad could talk about was sport. Sport. Out swingers, in swingers, layups, slam dunks. You hardly ever bothered to speak to me.

JIMMY: Look. You and I were never on the same wavelength. It's why we could never work together.

LUKE: I knew ten times as much as you did about our business. I could actually speak to our designers and engineers and understand their problems.

JIMMY: You had zilch management skills.

LUKE: You make a few jokes and get people laughing and you think that's management?

JIMMY: Have you seen last year's profits?

LUKE: You went to Dad and told him I had to go.

JIMMY: Stop obsessing about the past and do the right thing by your father.

LUKE: A father who fires me by letter?

JIMMY: To be honest I couldn't believe he'd done it that way. But he knows now it was a huge mistake and he's begged you to forgive him.

LUKE: It's more than that letter. It's our whole history.

JIMMY: Mate, stop fucking obsessing about the past and come to terms with what's happening now! If you ask me Dad has been unbelievably tolerant of the way you've been treating him. Despite not even being allowed to see his own grandkids he's never once suggested altering his will.

LUKE: I don't want his money.

JIMMY: You're one sick puppy Luke.

LUKE: I'm a sick puppy? Maybe you should take a look at yourself!

JIMMY: What've I done?

LUKE: How about bad-mouthing me to Dad behind my back instead of coming to me and saying, 'We have a problem here. We can't run this company together. What are we going to do about it?'

JIMMY: If we're going to 'sort' things out, admit it. Dad made the right choice!

LUKE: You both should still have talked to me.

JIMMY: Yes. We should've. Any other sins you want to lay on me?

LUKE: Trying to seduce Lauren in front of my bloody eyes? You think I could ever forget that?

JIMMY: A stupid drunken kiss in the garden. It didn't mean anything

> LUKE *turns away.*

How are things? Between you?

LUKE: Dire. She's having an affair and threatening to leave.

JIMMY: She's having an affair? That's outrageous

LUKE: She claims she's not but I'm ninety percent sure she's lying.

JIMMY: Ditch her. You'll find someone better.

LUKE: Attracted by my charisma?

JIMMY: Okay, you're a bit OCD but when it's not distorted by paranoia, your basic nature is decent.

LUKE: Decent?

JIMMY: Most older brothers give their younger brothers hell but you were always decent.

LUKE: Doing what?

JIMMY: You didn't mind me using your toys and if there was something I couldn't do you showed me.

LUKE *gets up and walks to the window.*

LUKE: Susy and the kids out today?

JIMMY: They've gone.

LUKE: Gone?

JIMMY: A three-bedroom apartment on the other side of the city. I stuffed up once too often.

LUKE: She'll come back. Surely.

JIMMY: No. I always assumed I could charm my way back but this time no. It's over.

LUKE: It's really that serious?

JIMMY: Yep.

LUKE: How are you coping?

JIMMY: I'm not. I've been drinking too much and wallowing in self pity.

JIMMY *wanders towards the window in silence then turns back.*

Dad wants me to help him kill himself before he wastes away.

LUKE *stares at him.*

LUKE: How?

JIMMY: Inject Nembutal.

LUKE: Isn't it illegal? Nembutal?

JIMMY: Very. I'll have to smuggle it through customs.

LUKE: Where are you going to get it?

JIMMY: Peru.

LUKE: You're okay with all that?

JIMMY: No, I'm not. It's a class A barbiturate and bringing it through customs can incur a jail sentence and a fine up to eight hundred and twenty-five thousand dollars! But Dad wants to go out with dignity and, unlike you, I care about him.

LUKE: That's the maximum for trafficking. You won't get that.

JIMMY: I'm supposed to take your word for that?

LUKE: Check it out online

JIMMY: I have. What I'm doing isn't euthanasia, which is illegal enough, but assisting suicide which is much more illegal. Here in New South Wales it's ten years jail.

LUKE: Get him to write his own suicide note.

JIMMY: He is.

LUKE: When are you going to Peru?

JIMMY: As soon as possible. Time's running out. Problem is I have the kids at the weekend. Could you at least help me out with that?

LUKE: It'd actually help me out if ours had someone to play with. Frankly I'm at my wits end trying to keep mine amused. They refuse to go to the zoo and the aquarium one more time, and Luna Park has totally lost its appeal.

JIMMY: Not easy is it.

LUKE: And the cartoons they watch.

JIMMY: Torture. Thanks mate. That'll help a bit. A warning about young Megan. She's a brilliant manipulator.

> *Beat.*

What's going to happen with Lauren?

LUKE: She'll divorce me eventually.

JIMMY: Don't dance to her timetable. Move out. Move on.

LUKE: To what?

JIMMY: To a woman who values you for God's sake. Stop all this pathetic beating yourself up. Go and look at yourself in the mirror. You're handsome—

LUKE: Handsome?

JIMMY: Not while you dress like a tramp and wear glasses that make you look like the local psychopath. Switch to contact lenses. And get a decent barber.

LUKE: Handsome?

JIMMY: Potentially. And fit. And wealthy. How many more assets do you need?

LUKE: Is my fashion sense that bad?

JIMMY: If I didn't know you and saw you in the street, I'd think we should be doing more for our homeless. [*Looking at his brother critically*] For fuck's sake go shopping. I'll take you. If you looked a little sharper you mightn't be such a miserable vindictive prick!

> *He looks at* LUKE's *head and frowns.*

Your hairdresser? Where did he do his training? In Nyngan, shearing sheep?

LUKE: He's cheap.

JIMMY: Of course he's fucking cheap. No-one would pay good money to have hair like yours! We'll get you a good hairdresser as well.

LUKE looks at himself in the mirror. He tries looking at himself from various angles. His facial expression indicates he doesn't like what he sees.

LUKE: I'd better go.

JIMMY: Okay, but listen to me. If you don't go and try and sort it out with Dad before he dies, I'll come and beat the shit out've you.

And LUKE *knows he means it.*

SCENE SIXTEEN

LAUREN *has come to visit* STEVE *in the living room of Steve's house.*

LAUREN: To be honest Steve, I think he's suffering some kind of mental breakdown.

STEVE: Really.

LAUREN: I know that this isn't the right time to be bothering you. You've got problems of your own.

STEVE: I can't deny that.

LAUREN: The whole family wants to see you pull through.

STEVE: I'm glad to hear you say that. When there's a lot of money involved some people would rather get their hands on it sooner rather than later.

LAUREN: I'm sure that's not how anyone in this family thinks.

STEVE: In Luke's case of course, I needn't worry because his is all going to cancer research.

LAUREN: It's certainly a nice thought to donate his money to—

STEVE: My money actually—

LAUREN: To charity.

STEVE: To cancer research. I was quite moved when he told me.

LAUREN: Yes it's a nice gesture but on the other hand he's robbing your grandchildren of a secure financial future.

STEVE: Ah, this is about my grandchildren?

LAUREN: Yes. I definitely think its a really worthy thing if some proportion of your money went to cancer research, but surely you'd die happier if you knew your grandchildren were well provided for in a stable marriage.

STEVE: He seems to have made up his mind.

LAUREN: Whilst respecting Luke's wishes, surely we can come to some arrangement that ensures your grandchildren are well looked after.

STEVE: And if you did divorce him you'd be executor?

LAUREN: If the worst does happen rest assured I'd spend it wisely on their behalf.

STEVE: And if you have a nice lifestyle the happier my grandchildren will be?

LAUREN: Yes. And you'd die knowing how grateful I was to you for that. And possibly that might make you a little happier too.

STEVE: Sadly Lauren, I'm not sure it would. I'll be encouraging Luke to stick to his guns, give my money to cancer research. I'm sure that between you, my grandchildren will be fine. Could you shut the door on your way out.

SCENE SEVENTEEN

LUKE *is angry as he confronts* LAUREN.

LUKE: You asked him to leave you money?

LAUREN: I asked him to leave our kids money, but he's not going to, so don't carry on.

LUKE: And I'm not changing my mind about the inheritance, so there's no need for you to stay married to me any longer.

LAUREN: You want our marriage to be over?

LUKE: It's already over. You've been fucking Murray Hendon for years! [*Angrily*] For once tell the truth!

> *Beat.*

LAUREN: I didn't mean it to happen.

LUKE: Are you going to live with him?

LAUREN: He wants me to.

LUKE: He becomes father to my children?

LAUREN: No! He doesn't want that! He's got four grown up children of his own.

LUKE: So how is this going to work? You dump the kids on me so you can go and live on the Riviera?

LAUREN: Luke I didn't plan for this to happen. I worked with him for months … we fell in love.

LUKE: With him or his share portfolio!

LAUREN: With him! It's not the money!

He strides offstage, angry.

Where are you going?

LUKE: [*offstage*] Packing!

LAUREN: You're leaving? Now? Right now?

LUKE: [*offstage*] Yeah!

LAUREN: What am I supposed to tell the children in the morning?

LUKE: [*offstage*] That their father loves them and will see them soon.

LAUREN *sits. Her phone rings. She looks at the dial.*

LAUREN: [*hushed*] Honey it's a bad time to talk. He's found out and he's walking out. No, no. It'll be fine. Yeah, sure he's angry. But it'll be fine. Look it had to happen and it's a relief that it has …

The door slams. LUKE*'s car roars off.*

He's gone. Yeah, it does change things. Murray, I'd love to go too Europe with you but I can't just leave the kids here if Luke won't take them. Yes I love you too, but please! It's far too early to make any plans now! Right now I just need get to sleep and we'll talk tomorrow.

LAUREN *ends the call and sits staring straight ahead.*

SCENE EIGHTEEN

In an exclusive and fashionable menswear shop in an arcade in the Queen Victoria Building, JIMMY *rather ruthlessly selects the jacket his brother should be wearing.* LUKE *is already in fashionable pants and shirt, and several other expensive shirts are ready for wrapping on the counter.* JIMMY *looks at the coat* LUKE *is wearing.*

LUKE: Looks good?

JIMMY *shakes his head, and helps him into another, then another and is finally satisfied.*

JIMMY: Right. Now shoes. Italian.

JIMMY *points down the arcade in the general direction of their next destination as a pleased the* SHOP ASSISTANT *takes the credit card* LUKE *is handing him.*

SCENE NINETEEN

LUKE, *stands in front of a mirror looking at his new fashionable clothes. He hears the doorbell, takes one last nervous look and hurries across to the door. He opens it and ushers in* SUSY. *She's even more surprised than he is.*

SUSY: Have you been on 'Queer eye for the straight guy'?

LUKE: I worked out that no woman would ever look at me if I didn't sharpen up.

SUSY: You're looking for a new partner?

LUKE: I don't intend to stay single for the rest of my life. How do you like my new pad?

SUSY: Stylish. Lauren? She's in Europe?

LUKE: Saint Tropez to be precise.

SUSY: And you've got the kids?

LUKE: With the help of a part-time housekeeper/childminder. A lovely old grandmother. Betty

SUSY: So when's Lauren coming back?

LUKE: Not sure.

SUSY: She's not missing the kids?

LUKE: They Skype.

SUSY: That's enough for her?

> LUKE *shrugs.*

LUKE: She's living her dream.

> SUSY *frowns. She obviously doesn't approve of* LAUREN's *behaviour but says nothing.*

Is it really all over with Jimmy and you?

SUSY: It takes a lot to get me to a decision point, but once I've made it, I've made it. Where are the kids?

LUKE: Still happily playing out the back.

SUSY: They're getting on well?

LUKE: Connie had a bit of a power struggle with Megan.

SUSY: Inevitable. Megan's the pushiest little seven year old I've ever seen.

LUKE: She's hilarious. The rules have to be absolutely spelled out before anyone starts the game. Do you want me to get them?

SUSY: No, let's just sit and talk for a while. I've had a hell of a week.

She flops into a chair.

LUKE: What happened?

SUSY: A couple I was supposed to counsel on their marital problems turned up totally smashed on ice and nearly killed each other. You wouldn't have any white wine would you?

LUKE: Oh er yes.

SUSY: Pinot Grigio?

LUKE: Pinot Gris.

SUSY: Near enough.

LUKE: I'll get it.

SUSY: Are you still refusing to talk to your father?

LUKE: What have we got to say?

SUSY: He may have some things to say to you.

LUKE: Like what?

SUSY: That if he has made mistakes, he's sorry for them.

LUKE: My father admit he'd made a mistake?

SUSY: You never know, he might surprise you.

LUKE *looks away.*

LUKE: Does he want to see me?

SUSY: Of course he does.

LUKE *says nothing.*

You were going to get me a Pinot Gris?

LUKE: Ah, yes.

He goes offstage.

SUSY: [*calling after him*] How's Jimmy?

LUKE: [*offstage*] Very cut up.

SUSY: He'll soon get over it and get out on the prowl again.

LUKE *comes back onstage with bottle and glasses.*

LUKE: No. He's in a mess.

SUSY: Really?

LUKE: [*pouring her and himself a drink*] Susy, any man who's not totally crazy would be cut up if they lost you. [*Off her reaction*] Sorry, just saying what I feel. I thought he was a total moron to go fooling around. I felt like shaking him and pointing to you, whacking him around the ears, and telling him he should be so lucky. [*Off her reaction*] Sorry, I've embarrassed you.

SUSY: No! You've just lifted me out of a month-long depression.

LUKE: I'm actually glad you've left him. He never deserved you.

SUSY: If you're going to pour don't be so stingy.

> LUKE *fills her glass.*

That's better. So it's all over with Lauren?

LUKE: Seems so.

> *Beat.*

Her father went bankrupt, lost the mansion, the Mercedes, and the Palm Beach weekender and she was hauled out of private school. She's been obsessed with money ever since.

SUSY: Seems that way.

LUKE: To be honest, I don't think we were ever right for each other. I'm a bit OCD, and not exactly the life of the party. Jimmy was always so good at being funny. I used to be insanely jealous.

SUSY: Guys like Jimmy are great in company but irritating to be married to. They're not really participating in a conversation, they're just waiting for the feed line for their next gag.

LUKE: He always made me feel like a klutz.

SUSY: If you're going to have any success with dating you're going to have to stop putting yourself down.

LUKE: I thought modesty was appealing?

SUSY: Modesty but not self-denigration. Stop it.

> *She looks at him sternly. He nods.*

LUKE: Do you think this sort of makeover … [*indicating his clothes*] might help me find someone?

SUSY: Clothes won't do it. It's about who you are and what you have to offer.

LUKE: So what do I have to offer?

> SUSY *ponders this point.*

SUSY: Those are great shoes by the way.

LUKE: The shoes are the only thing I've got going for me?

SUSY: No, I just noticed them.

LUKE: Italian. So my next good point.

   Beat.

   I'm waiting.

SUSY: You're a good listener.

LUKE: If you've got nothing to say it's your only option.

SUSY: People like good listeners.

LUKE: That's it? End of what I have to offer?

   SUSY *thinks.*

SUSY: Ordinary. You're ordinary.

LUKE: That's a good thing?

SUSY: Absolutely.

LUKE: Ordinary?

SUSY: Ordinary.

LUKE: Really?

SUSY: We've had enough of being fucked over by Mr. Charisma.

LUKE: You start looking for ordinary?

SUSY: Most sensible women do, but I stuck with Jimmy and look where that led.

LUKE: So now you're looking for ordinary?

SUSY: Yeah.

LUKE: Like me?

SUSY: Er—

LUKE: Not that ordinary?

SUSY: Some lovely woman out there will want you.

LUKE: But not you?

SUSY: Luke, that would be full on family drama of cataclysmic proportions.

LUKE: It was just a hypothetical. I was just trying to see if my level of ordinariness could ever attract someone as hot as you. Obviously not.

SUSY: I don't like that word, hot.

LUKE: Well you are. You're up there with …

SUSY: Who?

LUKE: Keira Knightley. I'm not trying to hit on you. I'm just stating things as I see them.

   SUSY *steals a glance at herself in the mirror.*

SUSY: Nice wine. Can I have some more?

> LUKE *pours it.*

LUKE: Nothing more to sell than ordinary?

SUSY: You've got a social conscience.

LUKE: Have I?

SUSY: You should. We all should. We need to be concerned at the state of the world. Inequality, war, refugees, climate change, sex trafficking.

LUKE: I could improve a little in that area.

SUSY: Depth. You read, don't you?

LUKE: Yes.

SUSY: Tolstoy, Jane Austen, Proust.

LUKE: Thrillers.

SUSY: Cinema. Wes Anderson, Jane Campion, Almodovar?

LUKE: Thrillers. I'm going to be a hard sell aren't I?

SUSY: Available.

LUKE: Available.

SUSY: Successful, available. Prepared to commit. Irresistible.

LUKE: How about something to eat? Feed the kids.

SUSY: Great idea. I was dreading going home and organizing all that. Any good takeaways around here?

LUKE: Sure, not being a good cook, first thing I checked out. Thai, Italian, Vietnamese, Chinese, Indian, Lebanese—

SUSY: What would you like?

LUKE: Thai?

SUSY: Too much sugar. Indian? My kids like it if it's not too spicy.

LUKE: I'll call.

> *He moves offstage.* SUSY, *already a little drunk, goes across to the mirror and sizes herself up.*

SUSY: Keira eat your heart out.

END OF ACT ONE

ACT TWO

SCENE TWENTY

JIMMY *is at* LUKE*'s place and he's furious.* LUKE *has another super fashionable shirt on which only makes* JIMMY *madder.*

JIMMY: I ring from Thailand to check on the kids and she's not there and the kids aren't there and I get worried and ring her friends and she's not there and I ring you and you calmly say, yeah she's here. She stayed last night with the kids.

LUKE: Hey, you don't own her mate. She's left you. She's a free agent.

JIMMY: I do the right thing. Take you out shopping. Make you look human and you sleep with my wife!

LUKE: I didn't sleep with her.

JIMMY: She woke up the next morning in your bed in her underwear.

LUKE: She asked me to take her dress off. She was worried it'd get crushed.

JIMMY: And nothing happened? You expect me to believe that.

LUKE: Nothing happened. She was drunk. I'd never take advantage of someone in that state.

JIMMY: Did she want you to?

LUKE: She was drunk.

JIMMY: Did she want you to?

LUKE: She was affectionate.

JIMMY: Affectionate.

LUKE: All I did was tuck her in.

JIMMY: And two days later you're having coffee with her? And again three days ago.

LUKE: In the day. In the city.

JIMMY: Why? If nothing happened, why?

LUKE: We like talking with each other.

JIMMY: About what?

LUKE: She told me I should see Dad.

JIMMY: You should. What else?

LUKE: The state of the world.

JIMMY: State of the world?

LUKE: Inequality, war, refugees, climate change, sex trafficking.

JIMMY: State of the world?

LUKE: And art and books and movies.

JIMMY: What books? What movies?

LUKE: Stuff with resonance and depth.

JIMMY: You're not interested in that. And she's not.

LUKE: You don't know your ex-wife very well, do you?

JIMMY: She's not an ex-wife. She's my wife.

LUKE: She wants a divorce.

JIMMY: I'm in Peru doing the right thing by Dad, and you're back here making a move on my wife.

LUKE: I'm not making a move on your wife.

JIMMY: Is this some sick idea of revenge on me? Get back at me for being—in your eyes at least—the favourite son?

LUKE: I'm not—

JIMMY: How low can you stoop.

LUKE: I'm not—

JIMMY: I take the trouble to show you how to dress and suddenly you're God's gift to women! Your brother's wife! You're a total sicko!

LUKE: I'm not seducing your wife!

JIMMY: If I thought—

LUKE: If you thought what—

JIMMY: That you and she—

LUKE: Why shouldn't she?

JIMMY: Because you're so bloody . . .

LUKE: What?

JIMMY: Ordinary!

LUKE: If you understood women a little better you'd realize you've just paid me a compliment.

JIMMY: What?

LUKE: Nothing's happening. Just get a grip on yourself.

JIMMY: Peru's a bloody disaster then I come home to this!

LUKE: What went wrong in Peru?

SCENE TWENTY-ONE.

JIMMY *is at* STEVE'S *place and* STEVE *isn't happy. Neither is* HELEN.

STEVE: Sniffer dogs?

> *He stares at* JIMMY.

How in the hell would sniffer dogs be able to smell Nembutal in a sealed bottle.

JIMMY: They must have picked up some other chemical type smell.

STEVE: What type of chemical smell.

JIMMY: I don't know.

> STEVE *sees* HELEN *looking skyward and rolling her eyes.*

STEVE: What's the real story?

JIMMY: I smoked a joint or two before I left Peru. There might have been some residual trace on my jacket or something.

STEVE: Oh Jesus.

JIMMY: They searched everything and found the bottle.

STEVE: Jimmy!

JIMMY: Sorry.

STEVE: I was totally counting on this. My weight's dropping already and I'm starting to feel really crook. Especially in the mornings.

JIMMY: Is anyone worried about what could happen to me?

STEVE: Jimmy don't carry on. We checked it out. You'll probably get a good behavior bond and no recorded conviction.

HELEN: But it does mean that if your father's found with Nembutal in his bloodstream—

JIMMY: That I'm the one who probably sourced it and I'd be charged with assisting suicide.

HELEN: [*to* STEVE] Exactly so there's got to be a clear electronic trail that shows you imported it yourself.

STEVE: I can't bloody travel.

HELEN: Online. There's a lot of scammers but Jimmy will do some research. Won't you Jimmy?

JIMMY: I'll try.

STEVE: Well try bloody hard will you son? Time's running out.

JIMMY: You can't trust those online sites.

HELEN: There's a euthanasia group who test it for you free. I'll help you find it. On Steve's computer and the electronic trail will only implicate you.

STEVE: How long will this take?

HELEN: If we can find the right supplier Express Post will get it here in days.

STEVE: Get onto it for God's sake.

He looks at his son and shakes his head in despair.

Smoking pot? Before you boarded the flight? You're the CEO of an international company, not some dropout who's stumbled in from Nimbin!

JIMMY: Okay, okay.

STEVE: And talking about being a CEO, Charlie tells me you're not turning up most days? To a company you're running? Okay, your marriage has broken down but it's no excuse for being missing in action. What the hell is up with you?

JIMMY: Ask Luke.

STEVE: Luke? Luke's got nothing to do with the firm.

JIMMY: He's dating my wife!

STEVE: What?!

JIMMY: I'm in Peru and he's back here making a move on my wife!

STEVE: Susy?

HELEN: You're joking?

JIMMY: She stayed overnight with him. With my kids. She slept in his bed!

STEVE: In his bed?

JIMMY: Yes.

STEVE: What the hell was she staying with him for?

JIMMY: So the cousins could get to know each other.

STEVE: Sounds like more than the cousins got to know each other.

JIMMY: My own brother. Jason told me that Uncle Luke was going to be their new daddy but I could be an uncle. And he looked happy!

STEVE *looks at* HELEN.

SCENE TWENTY-TWO

HELEN *is sitting down in a cafe with* SUSY.

HELEN: Susy this just can't go on.

SUSY: There's no drama.

HELEN: No drama? Jimmy would never recover.

SUSY: From what? That his brother and I are good friends.

HELEN: Staying over. Sleeping in his bed? I didn't come down in the last shower Susy.

SUSY: We're just friends.

HELEN: Let's say I believe you.

SUSY: Why wouldn't you?

HELEN: Sleeping in his bed?

SUSY: I drank too much and couldn't drive.

HELEN: Was Luke in the bed with you?

SUSY: No. I had a rough week. I drank too much. When I woke up he was sleeping downstairs on the sofa.

> HELEN *looks sceptical.*

Helen, truly, we're just friends.

HELEN: Is it going to stay that way?

SUSY: Absolutely.

HELEN: Your kids and Luke's kids are apparently planning for you to get married to each other.

SUSY: Helen. It's never going to happen. Luke's a nice guy, but he doesn't float my boat.

HELEN: Float your boat?

SUSY: Beat my drum. Truthfully. Set your mind at rest, it's never going to happen.

HELEN: I hope you can make Jimmy believe that. He's beside himself with rage.

SUSY: Yes, it's great.

HELEN: This is payback?

SUSY: He deserves it.

HELEN: Jimmy's really suffering.

SUSY: Like I was when he was cheating on me. You weren't concerned back then.

HELEN: I'm sorry.

SUSY: As far as you were concerned the sun shone out of your son's bum, and I should bask in the golden rays and remind myself how lucky I was.

HELEN: Mothers everywhere love their sons.

SUSY: And it gives daughters in law everywhere the shits. Sorry Helen. I'm sure you're better than most.

HELEN: If you had any heart you'd stop this business with Luke.

SUSY: Helen. I enjoy his company and that's it.

HELEN: Jimmy loves you desperately.

SUSY: Its taken him quite a while to work that out.

HELEN: He loves his kids.

SUSY: I know.

HELEN: And he'd love you to be a family again.

SUSY: I know. How's Steve?

HELEN: Not good.

SUSY: I'm sorry.

SCENE TWENTY-THREE

STEVE *sits in a chair looking out of the window of his apartment. He hears a noise and turns.* LUKE *stands there.*

STEVE: Luke. I wasn't expecting you.

LUKE: Sorry about your illness.

STEVE: Life's a bit like snakes and ladders. I had my fair share of ladders, but finally got the big snake.

LUKE: Sorry.

> STEVE *stands. He waits for* LUKE *to approach, but* LUKE *can't bring himself to hug his father.* STEVE *realizes this and indicates he should sit.* LUKE *does.* STEVE *sits opposite. There's a silence.*

STEVE: I'm sorry about the way you were let go from the company.

> LUKE *nods.*

It was a stupid mistake. I should've sat you down and talked.

LUKE: It wasn't just that.

STEVE: What was it?

> LUKE *looks at him.*

LUKE: I felt that to you I was almost … invisible.

STEVE: Invisible.

LUKE: With Jimmy you couldn't hear enough about what he'd been doing, what he was planning to do, what he was thinking— Question after question after question. With me? Zilch.

STEVE: Maybe that's because he was prepared to tell me. Getting anything out of you was like drawing blood from a stone.

LUKE: Because I knew you weren't interested.

STEVE: [*irritated*] How can you be interested in someone who's about as communicative as the bloody Sphinx!

LUKE: [*angry*] Everything he did was great. Everything I did you were ashamed of.

STEVE: How could I be ashamed of a son who was coming top of his class year after year?

LUKE: I wasn't scoring a hundred runs was I? Or breaking the state junior hundred metres butterfly record. Or scoring thirty-five points on the basketball court.

STEVE: I was proud of that and I was proud of you doing so brilliantly in your studies.

LUKE: When I was twelve you said to me, 'Your brother's nearly two years younger than you but he knows to look adults in the eye and answer when they ask questions. Not stare at his boots and mumble.'

STEVE: I was trying to teach you something important. First impressions are vital.

LUKE: All I learned from that was that I was hopeless compared to Jimmy.

STEVE: No you weren't. You got much better at looking people in the eye.

LUKE: Never as good as Jimmy though?

STEVE: No, never as good as Jimmy. Jimmy floats through gatherings like an angel fish through coral. Effortlessly but everybody notices. It's his gift. But you got better. A lot better. And that made me proud.

LUKE: I never felt you were proud.

STEVE: What did you expect? A bloody elephant stamp every time you did something good. I was proud.

LUKE: The only emotion I could ever spot on your face was irritation.

STEVE: Okay. I'm not the best social communicator in the world. What do you want me to say?

LUKE: To admit that Jimmy was your favourite by far.

STEVE: I valued you just as much as him!

LUKE: [*exploding*] Dad, tell the truth! Whenever Jimmy came into a room your face lit up. When I came in you barely registered.

STEVE *points to a photo.*

STEVE: Look. A photo of me with my arm around you on graduation day. That isn't exactly a scowl on my face. If my smile was any wider the top of my head would've fallen off.

LUKE: When I only got a second class honours in one subject one year you said 'Sounds like you've started to coast son.'

STEVE: I was so used to you getting first class honours.

LUKE: I'm doing a combined Engineering/Law degree, the toughest gig on campus, and Jimmy's doing a crap marketing degree—

STEVE: It wasn't a crap degree.

LUKE: Marketing? Learning to lie convincingly to sell shit products? While I'm doing something hugely challenging and I get one second class honours and you make me feel like I've failed!

STEVE: This is less about me than your own massive touchiness.

LUKE: When Jimmy graduated with a bare pass, not first class honours like I did, you sent him on a holiday to Europe with a no-limit credit card! I got a night out with you guys at a restaurant. Did I imagine that?

STEVE: I had to promise him that trip to get him to finish his degree.

LUKE: Why didn't you try taking him aside and telling him he'd better stop his drinking, womanising and partying, or you'd stop his allowance.

STEVE: I should've.

LUKE: But you didn't. Dumped his fiancée two weeks before the marriage, walked out on his first wife and has regularly cheated on poor Susy—

STEVE: I didn't condone any of that.

LUKE: You didn't condemn it either. 'That's just Jimmy.'

STEVE: I never said that.

LUKE: I overheard you Dad. Those were your exact words to Mum.

STEVE: I was only trying to calm her down.

LUKE: Susy is a gem. Any man would be lucky to have her.

STEVE: He realizes that now.

LUKE: Dad, don't rewrite history. You'd sit down and talk for hours with him about any sport you care to name. I tried to talk to you one day about how Hannibal almost brought the Roman Empire to its knees—

STEVE: I remember. It was interesting.

LUKE: I'd barely started when you got up to check out the footy scores and never came back.

STEVE: Let's be honest son. You never quite had the knack of making a story ... compelling.

LUKE: I wasn't telling an anecdote. It was a story of the greatest general in history.

STEVE: Then that's how you should've started it. 'Dad, I'm going to tell you a story about the greatest general in history.' Bang. Attention caught right at the start.

LUKE: Maybe your attention span is more at fault than my ability as a raconteur.

STEVE: Any more of my faults you'd like to lay on me?

LUKE: I tried so hard to be good at sport.

STEVE: And I was proud of that. I'd spend hours in the backyard teaching you to bat and bowl. Have you forgotten that?

LUKE: No, I really loved those moments.

STEVE: You weren't gifted, but you worked at it and got better. I was proud of that.

LUKE: The one time you did come to see me play, I was out for two and you yelled at me in the car on the way home. 'Don't you know by now you never chase a ball wide outside the off stump.' That's all you said all the way home.

STEVE: Well bloody hell. All those hours drumming the basics into you and you go out there and forget everything.

LUKE: I was terrified I'd fail so of course I did.

STEVE: I'm to blame again.

LUKE: It was all wasted effort. Jimmy had better hand eye co-ordination when he was still in his cot than I did at ten. I was never going to end up becoming a Jimmy.

STEVE: [*erupting*] No you weren't! You were going to end up a paranoid, carping, self pitying, pain in the bum!

LUKE: [*erupting*] You loved him to death and didn't give a shit about me! And I'm supposed to smile and pretend it's not happening!

There's a silence.

STEVE: Luke. On a scale of one to ten of parental love and affection with Jimmy scoring ten, what do you think you scored?

LUKE: With Mum? Ten. With you?

STEVE: Yes.

LUKE: About two.

STEVE: Luke—

LUKE: [*emotional*] I was only eight and I was being bullied viciously by a couple of eleven-year-old thugs and it was making my life hell so I told you and you know what you said? 'You're too thin skinned. Toughen up.'

STEVE: Luke.

LUKE: It's true. I was thin skinned. Still am. But there was surely a better way of dealing with what I was going through than your parrot chorus 'Toughen up, toughen up, toughen up!'

STEVE: I was on the phone to the headmaster the very next day telling him that if it didn't stop I'd come to the school and show him just how it felt like to be bullied. Didn't you ever ask yourself why it suddenly stopped?

LUKE *stares.*

LUKE: Why didn't you tell me?

STEVE: Because it wouldn't have done you any good to feel there was someone around who was going to solve your problems for you.

LUKE: I would've known you cared!

STEVE: All those hours in the backyard playing cricket? I didn't care? On a scale of ten did you really think you only rated two?

There's a silence.

This may come as a shock to you Luke but parents have favourites. You ought to know that. They pretend they don't but they do. Now that's not fair. But then life isn't fair. If it was there'd be no-one born in poverty or with a disability or with an ugly face. So here's the truth. You weren't wrong. Jimmy was my favourite. But where you were totally wrong was pitching yourself at two. Most kids who aren't favourites beat themselves up when they shouldn't. You were eight point five. Okay maybe after all this yelling tonight down to eight. But two? Come on, get a life.

He gets up and walks around.

When you went out for a couple of runs that day my heart bloody well bled for you. I all but cried. I really admired you trying so hard in our backyard practice and I wanted to see it pay off more than anything in the world. If I was mad at you in the car on the way home it was because I hated seeing you humiliated and crushed. I never wanted you to suffer that humiliation again.

There's a silence.

I could've handled that moment a lot better. I could've said, 'Don't let it get you down, you'll do better next time.' But the fact I'm a D-grade communicator doesn't mean I don't love you.

Beat.

Eight and a half is not as good as ten. But it's a hell of a lot better than two.

Another silence. LUKE *stands there with tears in his eyes. He nods. He comes across to his father and hugs him.*

You've been thinking I only rated you two all these years? No wonder you hated my guts.

Beat.

I'm sorry about the firing fiasco.

LUKE: You were right. He can sell what we're doing. I can't. And truthfully I'm much happier doing what I'm doing now.

A silence.

STEVE: You really want to give your share of my money to cancer research?

LUKE: Yes.

STEVE: Because you can't bear to take a gift from me?

LUKE: Dad. I'm doing well. I really don't need it.

STEVE: I got the distinct impression Lauren isn't very happy with that decision.

LUKE: She's not. Truth is she's gone for good and I'm relieved.

STEVE: This time look for someone who loves you.

LUKE: Is there anything to love?

STEVE: If I rate you eight and a half there has to be.

> LUKE *fights to stop tears forming in his eyes.*

Are you going to be there for me at the end or aren't you?

LUKE: I'll be there.

SCENE TWENTY-FOUR.

STEVE *is sitting with a blanket over his knees looking at a family album. Other albums he's already looked at are piled up next to him.* HELEN *is sitting beside him watching him turn the pages.* STEVE *stops, frowns and points to a page.*

STEVE: Where was this?

HELEN: Pretty Beach. We rented a holiday house for Christmas for a couple of years before we could afford a place of our own.

STEVE: I can't remember a thing about it.

HELEN: You were there.

STEVE: [*puzzled, irritated*] I can see that I was there but I can't remember a thing about it.

> HELEN *smiles.*

HELEN: Your mind was often elsewhere in those days.

STEVE: My mind was always bloody well elsewhere it seems. [*Turning the page*] Jimmy riding a bike.

HELEN: Yes.

STEVE: He looks about five.

HELEN: Yes. He was.

STEVE: I can't remember teaching him.

HELEN: You didn't. You drove back to the city for meetings.

STEVE: Who taught him?

HELEN: Sam Hallyer.

STEVE: Who's Sam Hallyer?

HELEN: He was our neighbour. Two up.

STEVE: What did he look like?

> HELEN *turns a few pages.*

HELEN: There he is, there.

STEVE *peers at the photo.*

STEVE: I sort of faintly remember him. He taught Jimmy to ride?

HELEN: And Luke.

STEVE: And Luke. A neighbour I don't even remember taught both our boys to ride a bike?

HELEN: He and his wife couldn't have kids. He came and mowed our lawn sometimes when you were off interstate.

STEVE: Shit. Learning to ride a bike is one of the great moments in a kid's life. I wasn't there? For both of them?

HELEN: We were in debt. You were working eighteen hours a day. At one stage we thought we were going to have to sell the house.

STEVE: [*turning pages*] How old were they there?

HELEN: Luke was about nine and Jimmy seven.

STEVE: That's Pretty Beach again?

HELEN: Yes.

STEVE: They're both swimming.

HELEN: Jimmy was body surfing by then.

STEVE: Who taught him that?

HELEN: You did.

STEVE: [*angry with himself*] I can't remember it at all. These are huge moments in a kid's life and I can't even remember. What kind of father was I?

HELEN: You were desperate to make us financially secure. And had some really big setbacks but you refused to give in. I was proud of you.

STEVE: You went to all the parents nights at school. I was always too busy.

HELEN: You went to one or two.

STEVE: You went to all their concerts.

HELEN: You went to some.

STEVE: [*picking up a new album*] Oh Migod.

HELEN: What?

STEVE: [*pointing at a photo*] You were so ... beautiful. Still are.

HELEN: Don't lie.

STEVE: So beautiful. What was happening here?

HELEN: You were taking me out. Our twelfth wedding anniversary. You got me a beautiful bunch of flowers and that turquoise necklace I still wear.

STEVE: Did you choose it?

HELEN: No, you did.

STEVE: Truly?

> STEVE *suddenly becomes very angry with himself.*

You remember perfectly. All the important moments in our lives and our boys' lives and I remember nothing.

> *He thrusts the photo album away from him.*

My mind was fighting battles, winning wars, obsessing about the past, dreaming of the future, but never where it should've been. In the present.

HELEN: Your hard work made our lives possible.

STEVE: [*still angry with himself*] My hard work was mainly for my glory. Mr Big. The success. The man they envied. The man the waiters jumped for.

> *He shakes his head in despair.*

I had a son who never believed I loved him. Can you believe that? Damaged his whole life because I didn't have the time or skills to let him know I cared.

HELEN: You did care.

STEVE: You really cared. For me. For the boys and for your friends. A friend got sick I'd just say, that's tough. You'd be round there comforting them and buying them little presents to cheer them up because you cared. You lived a hundred percent of your life. I just wish I hadn't wasted so much of mine.

HELEN: You were what you were. And I loved you for it.

STEVE: Honestly.

HELEN: Honestly.

STEVE: I hate the thought of leaving you all. And I hate the thought of leaving you most of all.

> *Beat.*

It's getting near time. Each day's getting harder and harder. Do you think the boys are going to be able to do it.

HELEN: I'll take these albums away. They only upset you.

> *She goes to collect them.*

STEVE: No. Leave them. I need to try and recover as much of it as I can.

She looks at him, tending towards tearful, nods and leaves.

SCENE TWENTY-FIVE

JIMMY *is visiting* LUKE. *He's agitated.*

JIMMY: I can't do it.
LUKE: You're going to leave it all to me?
JIMMY: Can't do it.
LUKE: This isn't about us!
JIMMY: Press the syringe that kills your father? I can't do it Luke.
LUKE: But I can?
JIMMY: You two weren't as close!
LUKE: It's going to be just as difficult for me to push that plunger as you.
JIMMY: I can't do it.
LUKE: So what are you going to tell Dad? Sorry, you're going to have to suffer for the next few months and die an excruciating death.
JIMMY: For fuck's sake, you do it— I can't!

LUKE *looks at him.* JIMMY *looks away.*

SCENE TWENTY-SIX

STEVE *is there in his chair. He's hooked up to his pain relief solution entering his arm through a canula.* JIMMY *is anxious, standing looking out of the window.* LUKE *is sitting closer to him.* HELEN, *upset, is furthest away, sitting in corner. Near her on a stand is a cello and bow. On a stand near the bed sits the syringe with the Nembutal solution loaded in it. Beside it is the handwritten note in which* STEVE *has testified that no-one aided his suicide.*

HELEN: I'm going to have to leave before it happens.

LUKE *goes across and hugs his mother.*

LUKE: We'll let you know when—
STEVE: [*anxiously indicating the cello*] You promised you'd play—
HELEN: I'll come back before it's …

STEVE: [*to his sons*] She's going to play the Goldberg Variations. They're special to me. I was a final year engineering student at Sydney and your mother was studying at the Conservatorium. I'd seen her for weeks in the student cafeteria and love at first sight—you've heard all this?

LUKE: Not from you.

STEVE: I finally plucked up the courage to ask her out and I was frankly stunned when she said yes.

JIMMY: Thank God she did or we wouldn't be here.

STEVE: I went to pick her up at the Con and she was in a practice room playing them. I didn't know what they were then of course. I'd barely heard of Johann Sebastian Bach. I was a total cultural ignoramus but I just knew that they were beautiful. And that she was beautiful.

    HELEN *nods, remembering. She kisses* STEVE *gently.*

HELEN: I'll be back when the boys call me.

    She leaves, distraught.

JIMMY: Dad I have to go too.

STEVE: What?

JIMMY: I can't handle it. I've talked this through with Luke. He'll do it.

STEVE: Jimmy!

JIMMY: Sorry.

    He heads for the door.

STEVE: Not just yet son. There's things I'd like to know.

    JIMMY *halts.*

Is there a moment in your lives you can remember where I was a really good father to you? Really good? One that lives in your memory?

    LUKE *and* JIMMY *look at each other.*

It'd be good to know there was at least one.

JIMMY: You taught me how to catch a wave.

STEVE: I barely remember it.

JIMMY: I couldn't get the hang of it. You were very patient. Then suddenly I took off at the right moment and zoom. All the way in. And you came bounding after me and you grabbed me by the shoulders and said 'You little beauty!'

    There's a silence.

STEVE: Luke if you can't think of one, don't worry.

LUKE: The school play. I was juror number two. Not a huge part but I thought I did okay. And you came racing round backstage and said 'Wow. I had no idea we had a Laurence Olivier in the family.' And I knew you meant it by the look of total surprise on your face.

STEVE: I said that?

LUKE: I was high for weeks.

STEVE: Good to know I occasionally did something right.

He indicates the syringe.

Detach the syringe driver and insert it into the line.

JIMMY: I have to go.

He does. STEVE *turns to* LUKE.

STEVE: Please.

LUKE *picks up the syringe.*

[*Indicating the note*] The note's there saying that none of you had anything to do with this. That I injected the Nembutal myself.

LUKE *nods.*

STEVE: I'm ready. I really am. I've led a pretty blessed life and I'm happy to go. Believe me. No hesitation. Press the plunger. I can't do it myself.

LUKE *hesitates.*

Right now Luke. Please, while I'm feeling good.

LUKE *hesitates, then connects the syringe and moves to put his finger on the plunger.*

STEVE: Count to three.

Beat.

Now.

LUKE *draws back.*

LUKE: Dad, sorry.

STEVE: Luke, please.

LUKE: Sorry.

LUKE *turns and leaves the room.*

STEVE: Luke!

But he's gone. STEVE *sighs. After a short while he reaches for the syringe himself, but can't bring himself to press it.*

[*Despairing*] Will someone please get this done!

HELEN *hears him and enters.* STEVE *looks at* HELEN.

STEVE: Please. It's time.

HELEN *walks slowly across and pushes the plunger.*

Thank you.

He nods at her. She watches him and nods back. Then she goes to her cello.

HELEN: Good bye my warrior.

HELEN *starts to play the Goldberg Variations. The sound brings* LUKE *and* JIMMY *back into the room. The music plays on.* STEVE *smiles as his eyes start to close.*

SCENE TWENTY-SEVEN

LUKE *waits in a city cafe. He looks up.* LAUREN *sits down.*

LUKE: Hi.

LAUREN: Hi.

LUKE: So how is life with the fabulously wealthy Murray Hendon?

LAUREN: Don't!

LUKE: Dream come true I would have thought.

LAUREN: Don't be such a prick.

LUKE: The villa in the Riviera? The maxi yacht in Saint Tropez? Complete with helicopter?

LAUREN: There was no helicopter.

LUKE: This was your dream. You could do anything you wanted.

LAUREN: After six months I ran out of things I wanted. And he sat there reading the Wall Street Journal and the Economist all day. It didn't work. Are you pleased?

LUKE: [*nodding*] Bordering on ecstatic.

LAUREN: Don't be so bloody smug. We all make mistakes.

Beat.

What we had was a lot better than I thought it was.

There's a silence.

LUKE: I think I should tell you. I've started a new relationship.

LAUREN: [*recoiling*] I'm not asking to come back!

Beat.

I just want to see more of the kids.

He nods his head.

I want to go back to fifty-fifty.

LUKE: I have to warn you they're still pissed off at you.

LAUREN: Are they still really angry?

LUKE: They'll get over it. They want a mother.

LAUREN: You're happy to go back to fifty-fifty?

LUKE *nods.*

LUKE: I'm relieved. The little horrors are making it totally obvious they don't approve of my new friend.

LAUREN: Really bad?

LUKE: Actually apart from that they're great. Once you get over the shock that kids attain adult levels of cunning by the time they're three and a half, you can cope.

LAUREN: How are Connie's tantrums?

LUKE: Ah they're getting better and Cassie is so—

LAUREN: What?

LUKE: Kind. She lost a piece of her jigsaw puzzle and was distraught, so I cut out some cardboard and coloured it but it was absolutely terrible. Then she found the missing piece and said, 'But thanks Daddy. Yours was really quite good.' I teared up.

LAUREN: That's beautiful.

LUKE: So what now for you?

LAUREN: Don't laugh but I'm moving into mediation.

LUKE: Good for you. What days do you want the kids?

LAUREN: Friday to Monday.

LUKE: The weekends? Good luck.

LAUREN: Hope your new relationship works out.

LUKE: Can't fail. I dress well, I'm ordinary, and I'm available.

LAUREN *doesn't quite know how to take this, but she eventually nods.*

SCENE TWENTY-EIGHT

JIMMY *sits alone at Luke's place drinking a glass of wine.* LUKE *enters and, as always now, is dressed very smartly.*

JIMMY: The cousins really do get on, don't they?

LUKE: They do.

JIMMY: You've got a new lady in your life I hear?

LUKE: Yeah.

JIMMY: How did you meet her?

LUKE: Tinder.

JIMMY: You're joking.

LUKE: I'd tried everything else.

JIMMY: She's not—

LUKE: She's terrific, she's got two kids of her own, but it's early days and we're taking things slowly.

JIMMY: I'm really glad for you mate.

> SUSY *comes in from outside.*

SUSY: How about you pour me a wine?

LUKE: Sorry.

SUSY: No, him.

JIMMY: Sorry.

> *He gets up and pours her a wine. He gives it to her.* HELEN *comes in from outside.*

HELEN: Those cousins get on unbelievably well.

SUSY: They really do.

HELEN: I've been dreading this day. A year since he died.

SUSY: You must miss him.

HELEN: Every day. Always will. Not quite sure why. He wasn't exactly an ideal husband.

LUKE: Or father.

HELEN: The truth was when I agreed to go out with him I already had a boyfriend.

SUSY: Really?

HELEN: A violinist at the Con. Talented, sensitive, musically and artistically literate, a great lover—

SUSY: What happened to him?

HELEN: He became principal violinist in the Berlin Philharmonic, married a German oboe player and is still over there with four kids.

JIMMY: Dad swept you off your feet?

HELEN: Anything but. He was so ignorant of the arts I felt sorry for him.

JIMMY: You dropped the violinist?

HELEN: No. I played a double game for about a year.

JIMMY: Really?

HELEN: I was a wicked girl back then. For a while I had three of them on the go and none knew about the others.

LUKE: Really?

SUSY: Why did you decide on Steve?

HELEN: I finally worked out my violinist was more in love with himself than with me, whereas Steve adored me. And he still did right to the end. It's hard not to love someone who adores you.

SUSY: Is there anything we can do?

HELEN: Being here with all of you is the very best thing you can do. [*Musing*] Stubborn, opinionated, insensitive, and artistically ignorant to the day he died.

JIMMY: He knew the Goldberg Variations.

HELEN: That's all he knew, believe me. To your father.

> *They drink a toast.*

LUKE: Will I order takeaway?

SUSY: Anything but Thai.

LUKE: Too much sugar, I know. You'd prefer the Indian. The one in Surry Hills not the one in Darlinghurst.

> JIMMY *looks at* LUKE *and* SUSY *suspiciously.*

[*Pointing to the couch*] I slept on the couch.

JIMMY: Okay, okay, very funny.

> JIMMY *turns to* SUSY, *still full of suspicion for confirmation.*

SUSY: I wouldn't know. I was drunk.

> JIMMY *glares back to* LUKE.

[*Teasing him, indicating* LUKE] I will admit it was a little hard to resist a man who dressed so well.

JIMMY *looks balefully at* LUKE.

HELEN: Susy, don't be so wicked. Jimmy stop worrying. Luke never lies. I know my sons. The cousins get on wonderfully. Susy has forgiven you—

SUSY: I haven't forgiven him.

JIMMY: I'm still on probation

HELEN: All is more or less well with the world.

> *She looks around all of them in turn. Puts a CD into the music player. It's Yo Yo Ma playing the Goldberg Variations. They sit down, sip a drink, and relax.*

THE END

www.ingramcontent.com/pod-product-compliance
Lightning Source LLC
Chambersburg PA
CBHW050025090426
42734CB00021B/3426